CW00516726

THE POETIC MEWS:
cats and their poets

Elizabeth Wager

with illustrations by
Gloria Cavicchioli

In memory of my mother
who first encouraged me to write poems
and with thanks to the friends
who continued this encouragement
and the cats who inspired these poems
and interfered with my typing

Contents

Foreword

Mary A. Turzillo,
author of Your Cat & Other Space Aliens
Cleveland, Ohio, USA

mary@maryturzillo.com

Touchstones of Literary Hiss-tory

If 'poets are the unacknowledged legislators of the world', as
Shelley maintains, then the history of the world can be seen
through literature. And how better to view history than through
the eyes of cats? This is the theme of Liz Wager's Poetic Mews.

Wager begins her tour of feline literature with Old English. Did
Beowulf have a cat? He certainly was acquainted with dragons,
so why would he not, after a long day of slaying monsters, have
sought the solace of a cat in his lap? And indeed, as Wager hints,
perhaps that dragon was something dreamed up by Beowulf's cat.
Or not.

She then turns to what might be called 'The Cat's Tale', except
that Chaucer's pilgrims left their felines at home to fend for
themselves. And, as with Chaucer's other tale-tellers, chastity is
not a leading virtue.

The leading figure in any history of English literature, and
therefore of the history of England and the world, would be
William Shakespurr, and Wager graces us with sonnets celebrating
both Will's own last will and testament and Falstaff's kitty, the
latter feline as much of a scapegrace as his master. Did the Bard
own a cat? How could he possibly have been as productive and
creative without one?

And so to blind Milton, and to amorous Marvell. The former
consoles himself with a puss, while the latter's cat administers
advice to would-be seducers.

Cruelty toward both humans and animals is a sad part of history,
and it is through literature that we learn of its effect on felines.
But in Wager's 'Ode to Hodge, after his Master', we enjoy Samuel
Johnson's more enlightened attitude. Hodge, Johnson's 'very fine
cat', has been celebrated throughout the centuries, and nowhere
more eloquently than here.

Cats are very musical, as we know even if we do not always appreciate their midnight serenades. So, a feline of W. S. Gilbert (the creative partner of Sir Arthur Sullivan) must have his say, as must Figaro's braggart ginger tom singing in Rossini's opera.

Valiant mousers are lauded as the quartermaster's cats in a Rudyard Kipling homage, and the notoriously excruciating verse in the style of William McGonagall shows that even bad poets may be fond of their cats.

Dylan Thomas's clowder is as disreputable as he, and pussycats of Edith Sitwell and John Betjeman each reveal the life style of early modern masters and their contemporaries.

Of course the comic tenor of the twentieth century (for all its disasters) must not be forgotten, and therefore we have an Ogden Nashish take on the commercialization of poetry.

The book ends with a poem that quite stands on its own -- as indeed do all the poems -- with an homage to a cat whose name we do not know. It is important to remember, as T. S. Eliot reminds us, that we never know the true name of our secretive, slinky pets.

Wager's mastery of poetry is as consummate as her regard for cats. Gerard Manley Hopkins' sprung rhythm, the Beowulf poet's alliterative accentual verse, Shakespurr's and Milton's sonnet form, the braggadocio arias of Beaumarchais/Rossini, the ballad form loved by Tennyson, Nash's light verse: Wager tackles all of them with relish and esprit, telling the tale of history, literary and otherwise, through cats.

I know you will delight in Wager's wit, whimsy, word-play, and sheer love of cats as much as I have. And perhaps this tour of feline literary history will illuminate what is most cat-like in our own history.

In sum, the connection between cats and literature speaks for itself in Archipuss No-Leash's poem.

Ars Felinica

by
Archipuss No Leash

A kitten should be risible and cute

with a pink snoot.

Warm

as a volcanic lifeform.

Silent when it stalks a catnip mouse,

then capering, destroy your house.

A kitten should not meow but purr

when mother licks its fur.

Pouncing, as the mother cat would pounce,

except with much more bounce,

pouncing on a bug, the wind, the moon,

or on a poem, or on last night's Tribune.

A kitten should be motionless asleep,

then purr and stretch and lick. Then it should leap.

A kitten should be equal to

a master of kung-fu.

For all the history of speed

a tumbleweed.

For love,

two manic eyes afire with glee.

A kitten's soul

is poetry.

Mary A. Turzillo

Beowulf's Cat

Lurking in long timbers, battle-scarred hero,

Ears irregular, ruin of rodents,

Agile athlete, ginger-furred guardian,

Whiskers a-bristle, alert for mouse murmurings,

Fish-scale scavenger,

Beowulf's cat ...

Often rested in rope tangles,

Sometimes sauntered on the slipway,

Vanishing into nightfall,

Meandered among mead benches,

Silent among feasting soldiers,

Darting between ankles, devouring dainties,

Gnawing bone and sucking sinew,

Licking lips luxuriously,

Then curled in corner comfort,

Gold-flecked pelt by flickering flame,

Remembering rat runs,

Dreaming of dragons.

The Complaint of the Pilgrims' Cat

Each year, in April, I am left for ages,
For that is when folk go on pilgrimages,
They chant their prayers and sing Magnificat,
But rarely give a thought unto their cat,
Their favourite hounds may join the merry throng,
But no one thinks of bringing cats along,
Full well they know that dogges cannot thrive
Without their master, yet cats stay alive.
Let fawning mongrels wait on man's command,
We cats prefer to take the upper hand,
Though we are smaller, yet we have more brain,
And therefore pilgrimage we do disdain.
We do not sing the Ave, Nunc or Pax,
We are too busy hunting tasty snacks,
If salmon, oysters, cream are gifts of God,
Refusal of such dainties does seem odd.
The nuns and friars take a rule of three:
Obedience, poverty and chastity,
We do not care to live upon a pittance,
Our law is wilfulness and lots of kittens.

Anne Hathaway's Cat Muses on Her Master

We are alone, a state we know full well;
Bereav'd, abandon'd, set aside at whim,
By fate deserted, yet by fame endowed,
Bound in eternity by links to him.
We were the minor players in his life,
Setting the scene, and yet by men unseen,
I was the playwright's cat, and you his wife:
Pursued in happier days when love was green.
Now our pursuit is simply to be fed;
He who could flatter men with words of gold
Left us no riches, just a time-worn bed,
A horde of poems and a love untol'd.
Though fate decreed that we should not be stars,
Our bed is second best, but it is ours!

Falstaff's Cat

In moonlight, along Windsor's alleys, there
I saunter past old triumph's former scenes.
Here's where I stole an oyster, there a hare,
See where I wooed a wench beside the streams;
And, like my master, I have honours won:
One ear a little torn, one hindfoot lame,
This eye, once sparkling, is forever gone,
Thus age has left its badges on my frame.
Our agile, sleek and handsome selves are chang'd
Into forms plumper, rheumy, aching, grey
Yet, in our minds, youth's beauty's not deranged
We are forever lissome, lithe and gay.
By day we drowse beside the embers' heat
And dream of battles fought and conquests made,
At dawn I will return to warm his feet
And rouse him with a gentle serenade.

Milton's Ode to His Pet

O sleek companion of my sightless days,
A velvet comfort in a world unlit,
Who nimbly 'pon my knees would leap and sit,
Content and peaceful with my confin'd ways.
As swift to greet at dawn or by star's rays,
When Sun and Moon my own dull life had quit.
If hours hung heavy, I lackt patience, yet
You taught me virtuous calm and silent praise.
But oft your ghostly gliding did me fright,
No phantom could so instantly appear,
Against my sleeve a sudden stroke of fur,
Surpris'd me from my sombre world of night.
In truth, good friend, I had no need to fear,
They also serve who only sit and purr.

Andrew Marvell's Cat Advises His Master

Had you but sense enough, and wit,
You would not languish in this fit.
You would sit down and watch the way
I sleep and purr throughout the day.
You would not fly to Ganges' shore,
Or drive each day an hour or more,
You would not check your phone each second
To see if your amour had beckoned.
Watch my methods, foolish chap,
The secret to your lady's lap
Is lull her with a soothing purr
And offer her your softest fur,
Nuzzle her gently with your head,
But do not haste into her bed.
I agree, her lap is nice,
But what's the rush? Take my advice,
Carpe diem (seize the day)
Is your watchword, critics say,
Cats prefer a phrase less sharp ...
Carpe diem? Eat more carp.

An Absent Cat from History

In old King Charles's glorious days
Upon the throne he sat,
A fawning spaniel at his feet --
He should have had a cat.
Cats do not care if you are king
For they're already regal,
They do not do obedience
Like labrador or beagle.

A Sonnet to Hodge

Like my best books, I dwelt inside a case
And used my wit as a protective shell;
I flattered no one in the human race
And solitary in my life did dwell.
I let the harmless drudgery consume my days
And did not care for men's opinions or their praise.
And yet, dear Hodge, I could not bear with ease
That baleful look, the bristling up your spine,
When I denied your fineness, just to tease
That prattling fool who found the whole world fine;
For you, I changed my tenor, to concede
That yes, you were, a very fine cat indeed.

The Song of Hiawatha's Kitten

As the dawn lit up the forest,
As the forest birds were stirring,
When the mist rose off the meadow
And the sun rose up to greet her,
Hiawatha heard a rustling,
Heard a sound like thunder rolling,
Heard a deep unearthly growling,
Put his head under the pillow,
Pulled the buckskin to his eyebrows,
Dozed again, the sleep of heroes.
Woke again, an hour later,
When the sun had warmed the teepee;
Put a toe outside the buckskin,
Could not find his leather slippers,
Wandered round the teepee, bleary,
Cursing last night's firewater,
Left the flaps closed 'gainst the sunlight,
Could not bear the streaming sunlight,
Could not bear the noisy bluebirds.

Irritable Hiawatha,

Staggered from his cosy bedding,

Wondered where he'd left his slippers,

Felt a nasty cold sensation,

Oozing up around his toenails,

Felt a wetness, something squishy,

Sticking to his hardened foot soles,

In the darkness tried to wipe it,

Tried to lose the slimy feeling,

Tried to dry his sticky toenails,

Tried to clean his mucky foot soles.

Then, at last, he found a slipper!

Shoes of doeskin from his childhood,

(Moccasins his mother made him

To protect his feet from evil)

Joyful shoe of beaded doeskin,

Lying in an odd position,

Joyfully he thrust one foot in,

Thrust one foot into the slipper;

Hopping gently on one slipper,

Opened up the flaps of teepee,

Let the golden sunlight flicker,

Let the golden sunlight show him,

Half a mouse upon the doeskin,
Half a mouse with innards gory,
That was what he must have stepped in!
Felt a little queasy shudder,
Then beheld the other slipper,
Hopped on one foot round the teepee,
Hopped until he reached the slipper,
(Moccasin his mother made him
To protect his feet from evil)
Poked a toe into the slipper,
Felt the warm and furry lining,
Put his foot a little further,
Felt a ghastly sticky wetness,
Felt the feel of other mouse half.
Threw the slipper at the kitten,
Threw away his doeskin slipper,
Missed the cat, but hit the bottle,
Knocked the precious firewater,
Wasted all the fiery spirit,
Made the teepee really soggy,
Incandescent Hiawatha,
Head now pounding, stomach churning,
Cursed his luck and cursed the kitten,
Headed bedwards, feeling groggy.

The Lady of the Lap

by
All-furred Loud Tunny-Song

Within this verse we sing the praise
Of gentle lady, she who stays
And spends with us the Christmas days,
The Lady of the Lap.

There she knits by night and day
With winding wool in colours gay,
And with the needles lets us play;
We like it when she comes to stay,
Sweet Lady of the Lap.

We will not ever scratch or hurt,
We'll wash our paws quite free from dirt,
We love the hollow in her skirt,
To have a little nap.

On the sofa, cushions plump,
Drowsily in dreams we slump,
In a tortoiseshelly lump;
Only if you sneeze we'll jump
And run out of our flap.

Lovely lady please remain
For a longer visit when
We can snuggle up again,
Dear Lady of the Lap.

Figaro's Cat

Bravo bravissimo,
Generalissimo,
Mousing pianissimo,
Figaro's cat!
Nothing is furrier,
Nothing is purrier,
Never a hurrier,
Figaro's cat.
Dozing on periwigs,
Dreaming of sailing brigs,
Dining on stolen figs,
Figaro's cat.
Suckled 'neath scissor snips,
Pouncing on kirby grips,
Leaping at ribbon tips,
Figaro's cat.
Warm by the curling tongs,
Weaving through pavement throngs,
Filling the night with songs,
Figaro's cat.
Gingery, whiskery,
Stripey and friskery,
Dandy-odiskery
Figaro's cat!

The Lament of Mr Gilbert's Cat

I am the perfect specimen of feline infelicities,
I'm forced to earn my living so I have no chance to live at ease,
I chase marauding rodents far from Kensington to Hammersmith,
But rarely get to Billingsgate to taste a fish or have a sniff.
I sleep upon the piano stool or inside the harmonium,
The racket in the Gilbert house is sometimes pandemonium,
I'd suit a calm philosopher – a stoic or empiricist,
I don't know what I did to end up living with a lyricist!

His operatic lyrics are a masterpiece poetical,
To criticise his scansion you would have to be heretical,
His rhymes are quite preposterous regardless of modality,
But when it comes to feeding time he lacks in punctuality.
Although he's very famous, with his Gondoliers and Ruddigores,
It doesn't make him tolerant of moulting fur or muddy paws,
I scarcely dare to whisper but I fear I may have caught some fleas,
I am the perfect specimen of feline infelicities.

On the Sad Death of Mr McGonagall's Pet

Oh, glorious Tibbles who has passed away,

Alas, I am very sorry to say

That I shall no longer stroke your fur,

Or, in the night-time listen to you purr;

For the Lord has decreed that your time on earth should come
to an end:

And I must say, I have lost a very dear friend!

It should be recorded that you were the best of mousers,

Though once you jumped up and almost tore my trousers,

But you kept our household most wonderfully free from vermin

For which we all say a devout and heartfelt 'Amen'.

For, before you arrived, the mice would run riot,

And with scrabblings in the skirtings they were rarely ever quiet,

And although we invested in mousetraps of every make and size,

In November, several mice nibbled one of Mrs McGonagall's pies.

But now, alas, the McGonagall residence is pet-less,

And Mrs McGonagall is almost witless,

And I have to admit that my heart in twain is quite smitten,

So I must take the train to Dundee and immediately purchase
a kitten.

Furry Faithfulness

Glory be to God for tabby paws --

For subtle silver shimmer in a wash of grey;

For burnished tortoiseshell and ginger swirls;

Lithe-leaping supple spines; piercing claws;

Coalside drowsing and dreams -- a twitch, and pounce on prey;

And milk-crate rumbles, purr, rattle and furl.

All cats contrary, wary or absurd;

Whoever is furry-faithful (who can say?)

Who vaults the moon in starshine tumble turns;

With dawn-drenched whiskers diving for a bird:

Adore him!

The Ballad of the Quartermaster's Cats

Oh those scribblin' clerks in London 'aven't got a bloomin' clue,

Stuck behind their desks in Whitehall what the quartermasters do,

'Ow they guard the Queen's possessions: beer an' vittels, boots an' 'ats

And the quite essential function o' the quartermasters' cats.

Mr Monty is a mouser off the streets of Mandalay,

An' 'e works for Queen and country for a bowl o' milk a day,

Though 'e lost an eye in battle with them thieving Burmese rats,

'E's the tabby Major General of the quartermaster's cats.

Sergeant Barty was a kitten when 'e volunteered 'is paw,

An' 'e keeps a watchful eye on all them rations in the store;

'E may look as if 'e's sleepin' when he's curled up on the mats --

But at night he's scout and lookout for the quartermaster's cats.

Corporal Reggie is a veteran of the battle of the kegs,

An' 'e fiercely guards the storeroom, though 'e's only got three legs,

But 'e don't demand no pension 'cept a tickle an' a pat,

Every night 'e does his duty as a quartermaster's cat.

Now them old Whitehall accountants (just to show they still had guts)

Said they'd spotted 'inefficiencies' and had to make some cuts;

They accused the quartermaster of 'wasting food on pets'

And some toffee-nosed young captain said 'He's far too many cats'.

Now at this, the quartermaster was deflated, looked quite glum,

Said 'e couldn't do 'is duties, if 'e 'adn't got a chum,

So we 'id for the inspection in the space behind the slats,

An' you couldn't see a whisker o' the quartermaster's cats.

So we lurked up in the roofspace and we didn't make a sound,

Every single cat had vanished when the auditors came round,

Though we left a rat decaying and mouse droppings on the chair,

But in terms of feline residence they couldn't find a hair.

Now that night we did reconnaissance and scouted round the camp,

Barty dodged the old nightwatchmen and his interfering lamp,

An' 'e crept into the office while the staff were in their beds --

An' they haven't got a clue why that report is now in shreds.

But the Colonel likes 'is stilton with some crackers on a board --

And you should 'ave 'eard 'is language when 'e saw that they'd
        been gnawed,

So you office boys in London in yer bowlers and yer spats,

Just remember who's in charge 'ere – it's the quartermaster's cats.

Miss Sitwell's Cat

My purr is a velvety hurdy gurdy,

My lissome limbs are stalactite sturdy,

My eyes can pierce the stygian gloom,

Through Beelzebub's mansions, Hector's tomb.

My sable fur is treacle dark,

My claws are stilettos in the park,

Witchery whiskering twitching tail,

Daphnis and Chloe stole the milk pail.

Sleek, like the Queen of Sheba, I

Rule my realm with a yawn and a sigh,

Spurning the vermin, mouse or rat,

I am Edith Sitwell's cat!

If Ogden Had a Cat

Rhymes for tabby
Tend to be flabby,
But verses on tortoiseshell
Definitely oughtasell!

How to Get on in Feline Society

Watch for that salmon skin, Stanley
I very much fear it's been farmed;
You know I prefer the organic,
I don't want my appetite harmed.

Oh, is that a morsel of gruyere?
I'll sample it, if it is ripe.
Have you checked the French bistro for offal?
I fancy some sweetbread or tripe.

I cannot abide TV dinners
These humans have terrible taste,
Their food's over-processed and salty
And think of the packaging waste!

This bin is a gourmet disaster,
All microwaved rubbish and tins;
I do miss the local fishmonger's
Delectable skate tails and fins.

It's a pity the butcher is closing,
But nowadays nobody cooks;
Yet they watch all the cookery programmes
And always buy Delia's books.

This neighbourhood's clearly declining,
The children look pasty and fat;
While I'm getting thinner and thinner --
It's hard on a stray, gourmet cat.

The Cats of Milk Wood

It is dawn under Milk Wood

and the town's grandees are returning home

after a night of noisy carousing

dainty among milk bottles

whiskering along windowsills

as the town sleeps.

While, on steps glistening like new bicycles,

Mrs Tabby (Number 17, Fisherman's Row) pauses to talk to

Mrs Tabby (Number 4, Kipper Lane) to discuss

that no-good tortoiseshell at number 30

who's having kittens – again

and not sure who the father is – she never is!

and what does she want with more kittens?

Look. Behind the Sailors' Arms,

back from his night of beer and rat-catching,

the one-eyed ginger landlord greets a bloody-eared warrior

to lick his wounds and discuss the price of haddock

and did he notice the light's still on in that visitor's room

and the boyo is always writing

clackity-clacking the typewriter keys,

and he was drunk last night – but that doesn't stop him.

Wonder what he's writing?

Nobody ever writes about cats ...

And the curly-headed tomcat poet

stubs out another cigarette and writes about

the cats, napping in the slant corners

or streaking and needling on the one cloud of the roofs.

To an Unknown Poet

You do not know my name – I ask not yours;
You call me Tiddly Puss or Kitty Paws,
The name my mother used you never heard,
The special kitten whisper that she purred.
And p'rhaps it's best that you cannot translate
The midnight yowls of my seductive mate
Who summons me to trysts beyond the fence,
As his endearments might cause you offence.
So you don't know my name? Well, do not fret,
We do not share man's need for etiquette.
Doctor or Duchess, Baroness or Graf,
Cats treat all humans equally: as staff.
Famous or not, your laps we'll vault upon,
Even a laureate is to cats 'Anon'.